Kids' Travel Guide
Italy

FlyingKids® Presents:
Kids' Travel Guide
Italy

Authors: Elisa Davoglio & Shiela H. Leon
Editor: Carma Graber
Graphic Designer: Neboysha Dolovacki
Cover Illustrations and design: Francesca Guido
Published by FlyingKids® Limited

Visit us @ www.theflyingkids.com

Contact us: leonardo@theflyingkids.com

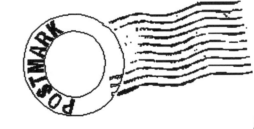

ISBN: 978-1-910994-02-3

Acknowledgement:
All images are from Diomedia and public domain except those listed below:
Dollar Photo Stock: 14bc, 15bc, 21m, 22m, 30mbcl, 30mbcr, 30mr, 32bc, 38mb.
Shutterstock: 15mb, 15mt, 29m1, 29m2, 29m3, 29m4, 29m5, 35bg, 37bg.
Attribution: 17mt-By Maurice Sand [Public domain], via Wikimedia Commons, p26m- By Roberto Vicario (Roberto Vicario) [CC BY-SA 3.0 (http://creativecommons.org/licenses/by-sa/3.0)], via Wikimedia Commons.

Key: t=top; b=bottom; l=left; r=right; c=center; m=main image; bg=background

Table of Contents

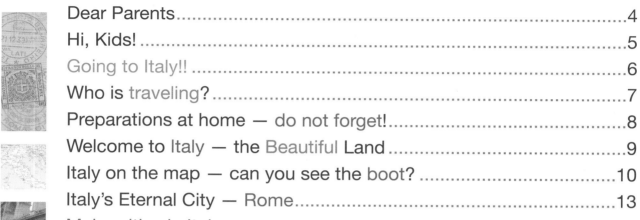

Dear Parents,

If you bought this book, you're probably planning a family trip with your kids. You are spending a lot of time and money in the hopes that this family vacation will be pleasant and fun. You would like your children to learn a little about the country you visit — its geography, history, unique culture, traditions, and more. And you hope they will always remember the trip as a very special experience.

The reality is often quite different. Parents find themselves frustrated as they struggle to convince their kids to join a tour or visit a landmark, while the kids just want to stay in and watch TV. On the road, the children are glued to their mobile devices instead of enjoying the new sights and scenery — or they complain and constantly ask, "When are we going to get there?" Many parents are disappointed after they return home and discover that their kids don't remember much about the trip and the new things they learned.

That's exactly why *Kids' Travel Guide — Italy* was created. With *Kids' Travel Guide — Italy*, young children become researchers and active participants in the trip. They learn fun facts about history and culture; they play games and take quizzes. This helps kids — and parents — enjoy the trip a lot more!

How does it work?

A family trip is fun. But difficulties can arise when children are not in their natural environment. *Kids' Travel Guide — Italy* takes this into account and supports children as they get ready for the trip, visit new places, learn new things, and finally, return home. The *Kids' Travel Guide — Italy* does this by helping children to prepare for the trip and know what to expect. During the trip, kids will read relevant facts about Italy and get advice on how to adapt to new situations. *Kids' Travel Guide — Italy* includes puzzles, tasks to complete, useful tips, and other recommendations along the way. All of this encourages children to experiment, explore, and be more involved in the family's activities — as well as to learn new information and make memories throughout the trip. In addition, kids are asked to document and write about their experiences during the trip, so that when you return home, they will have a memoir that will be fun to look at and reread again and again.

Kids' Travel Guide — Italy offers general information about Italy, so it is useful regardless of the city or part of the country you plan to visit. It includes basic geography; flags, symbols, and coins; basic history; and colorful facts about the culture and customs of Italy. If you are traveling to Rome, you may also want to get the *Kids' Travel Guide — Rome*, which focuses on the city itself — its history and culture, and all its interesting and unique attractions.

Ready for a new experience?
Have a nice trip and have fun!

Hi, Kids!

If you are reading this book, it means you are lucky — you are going to **Italy**!

You probably already know the places you will visit, and you may have noticed that your parents are getting ready for the journey. They have bought travel guides, looked for information on the Internet, and printed pages of information. They are talking to friends and people who have already visited **Italy,** in order to learn about it and know what to do, where to go, and when … But this book is not just another guidebook for your parents.

This book is for you only — the young traveler.

First and foremost, meet Leonardo, your very own personal guide on this trip. Leonardo has visited many places around the world. (Guess how he got there?) He will be with you throughout the book and the trip. Leonardo will tell you all about the places you will visit — it is always good to learn a little bit about the country and its history beforehand. He will provide many ideas, quizzes, tips, and other surprises. Leonardo will accompany you while you are packing and leaving home. He will stay in the hotel with you (don't worry, it does not cost more money)! And he will see the sights with you until you return home.

Have Fun!

A Travel Diary — the beginning!
Going to Italy!!!

How did you get to Italy?

By plane / ship / car / other _____

We will stay in Italy for _____ days.

Is this your first visit _____ ?

Where will you sleep? In a hotel / in a campsite / in a motel / in an apartment /
with family / other _____

What places are you planning to visit?

_____

_____

_____

What special activities are you planning to do?

_____

_____

_____

Are you excited about the trip?
This is an excitement indicator. Ask your family members how excited they are (from "not at all" up to "very, very much"), and mark each of their answers on the indicator. Leonardo has already marked the level of his excitement …

not at all   very,
                                                    very much

Leonardo

Who is traveling?

Write down the names of the family members traveling with you and their answers to the questions.

Paste a picture of your family.

Name: _____

Age: _____

Has he or she visited Italy before? yes / no

What is the most exciting thing about your upcoming trip?

_____
_____
_____

Name: _____

Age: _____

Has he or she visited Italy before? yes / no

What is the most exciting thing about your upcoming trip?

_____
_____

Name: _____

Age: _____

Has he or she visited Italy before? yes / no

What is the most exciting thing about your upcoming trip?

_____
_____

Name: _____

Age: _____

Has he or she visited Italy before? yes / no

What is the most exciting thing about your upcoming trip?

_____
_____

Name: _____

Age: _____

Has he or she visited Italy before? yes / no

What is the most exciting thing about your upcoming trip?

_____
_____

Preparations at home — DO NOT FORGET ...!

Mom or Dad will take care of packing clothes (how many pairs of pants, which comb to take …). Leonardo will only tell you the stuff he thinks you might want to take on your trip to Italy.

Here's the **Packing List** Leonardo made for you. You can check off each item as you pack it:

- ☐ *Kids' Travel Guide — Italy* — of course!
- ☐ Comfortable walking shoes
- ☐ A raincoat (One that folds up is best — sometimes it rains without warning …)
- ☐ A hat (and sunglasses, if you want)
- ☐ Pens and pencils
- ☐ Crayons and markers (It is always nice to color and paint.)
- ☐ A notebook or a writing pad (You can use it for games or writing, or to draw or doodle in when you're bored …)
- ☐ A book to read
- ☐ Your smartphone/tablet or camera
- ☐ _____
- ☐ _____

Welcome to Italy — the Beautiful Land

Italy is a magical place. Every year more than **40 million people** come to explore **Italy's many treasures**. It's one of the most popular countries to visit in the world — and you'll soon find out why!

In Italy, you can get an up-close look at fascinating history and famous art and monuments. You'll find exciting cities, beautiful scenery, wonderful beaches, lots of delicious food … and more.

Italy's nickname is *Belpaese* — Italian for "beautiful land."

Leonardo can't wait to tell you all about this great country. Let's get started …

Who knows which continent Italy is on? (Answer on the next page.)

Did you know?
Inside the country of Italy there are two independent nations: **Vatican City** and **the Republic of San Marino.**

The Republic of San Marino is one of the smallest countries in the world. It measures only **61 square km** (or **23¹/₂** square miles)!

Vatican City is located inside the city of Rome. It's the smallest country in the world: **0.44 square km** (or about 0.17 square miles). It is governed by the Pope, the head of the Catholic Church 😮.

Did you know?
Italy has over 3,000 museums.

ROATIA
Dubrovnik
Bari
Brindis
Taranto Lecce
Golfo di Otrant
Taranto
Sardini
Cosenza
Cagliari
Catanzaro
ISOLE EOLIE

Italy on the map —
can you see the BOOT?

Italy is easy to recognize on the map!
It is located in western Europe.
It's a peninsula — so it is bordered by the sea on three sides.
And Italy has the unusual shape of a boot!

A boot   Italy

What is a compass rose?

The compass rose is a drawing that shows the directions: North-South-East-West. North is always at the top of the map, and from that you can find the other directions. When you need to get to a place, you can use a compass. A compass rose is drawn on the face of the compass, and the needle always points North. This helps you to navigate and figure out what direction to go — so you can get from one place to another.

Mark the three missing directions in the blank squares.

North

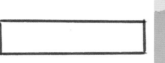 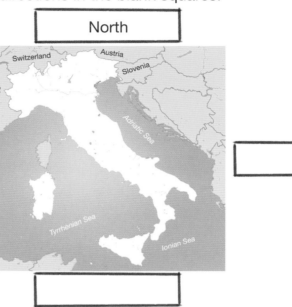 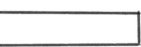

Italy is surrounded by several neighboring countries and seas. Can you find them on the map? Try to complete the following:

To the south _____

To the east _____

To the north _____

To the west _____

Italy's **beautiful** borders

Did you know? Borders were invented to separate different countries. A border is a line that marks the end of one country's territory and the beginning of another. There are all kinds of borders. Sometimes a river or a mountain range makes a natural border. And sometimes a fence or a special gate marks a border.

In Italy, there is a natural border to the north: the Italian Alps. These mountains separate Italy from the European countries of France, Switzerland, Austria, and Slovenia.

Italy is also bordered by the sea, and the country has two islands. What are they?

- Canary Islands
- Peter Pan Islands
- Sicily and Sardinia Islands

Answer: Sicily and Sardinia Islands

You are about to visit the beautiful cities of Italy. Can you find 10 cities in the word search puzzle?
- ✓ ROME
- ✓ FLORENCE
- ✓ VENICE
- ✓ PISA
- ✓ MILAN
- ✓ NAPLES
- ✓ PALERMO
- ✓ GENOVA
- ✓ PADOVA
- ✓ TORINO

R	A	O	I	E	N	C	E	A	M	F	G
E	O	R	D	S	G	Y	J	P	I	S	A
Q	E	M	U	S	K	Z	K	M	L	W	O
H	O	V	E	N	I	C	E	A	A	G	D
A	N	F	Z	F	L	O	R	E	N	C	E
C	A	M	X	L	O	R	I	N	Q	E	O
P	A	L	E	R	M	O	R	I	N	O	O
Y	D	S	G	I	R	K	Z	K	S	H	D
P	A	L	E	R	M	O	T	K	H	A	T
F	R	U	N	A	P	L	E	S	D	D	A
B	O	T	O	R	I	N	O	K	E	R	T
T	K	Z	V	A	N	S	I	E	S	Y	U
O	V	P	A	D	O	V	A	C	K	S	P

Italy's Eternal City — Rome

Italy has some of the most famous cities in the world. Fly around with Leonardo and learn about a few of them.

Rome is the capital of Italy! It is also called **the Eternal City,** because of its long history. It was the home of the ancient Roman Empire. This huge empire ruled for more than 1,000 years. During that time, the empire spread its beliefs and practices throughout the known world.

In Rome, there are many monuments — like the Colosseum, the ancient Forum, and the temples. They recall Rome's glorious past. That's why Rome is also called … (Choose the right answer below):

- The open-air museum
- The virtual museum
- School every day

Answer: Open-air museum

Quizzes!

Do you know which Italian city has the most people? A clue … It's also the capital!

- Milan
- Florence
- Rome

Answer: Rome, with a population of nearly three million.

Find the city of Rome on the map. Which sea is closest to Rome?

Answer: Tyrrhenian Sea

Florence — famous for art!

Florence is famous for being the city where many great Italian artists were born and lived during the "Renaissance."* Have you heard of artists like **Leonardo da Vinci**, **Michelangelo, Giotto, Raphael**, and **Botticelli**? They all lived in Florence and created wonderful pieces of art that you can still see today — like the **Tower of Giotto**!

*Renaissance is French for "rebirth." The Renaissance period started in Florence around the years 1350 to 1400. The Renaissance was a time of rebirth for knowledge. There was a lot of new growth in the arts, architecture, and science.

In those days, roads weren't paved … Florence was actually the first city in all of Europe to have paved roads and streets! They paved the streets by covering the ground with bricks or little flat stones. That made walking and driving carts easier and more comfortable.

The Giotto "O" There is a funny legend about the artist Giotto. The Pope wanted to find out whether Giotto was a good enough painter to work for him. So the Pope asked to see some of Giotto's paintings. But Giotto refused to show them to him. Instead, Giotto simply drew a perfect circle, like a big "O." The Pope was impressed. He decided that only an extraordinary painter could have drawn a circle that perfect! And that's how Giotto began to paint for the Pope …

Challenge your family to a contest! Imitate Giotto and see who can draw the best "O"!

Milan — great SHOPPING and high FASHION!

Remember when Leonardo told you that Italy is shaped like a boot? Well, Milan is located in the upper part of the boot — in northern Italy. It is the second largest city in country. One-and-a-half million people live there!

Milan is Italy's shopping capital. It is famous worldwide for its fashion, and has some of the best shops in Europe. There are even places to find high style at bargain prices.

In Milan, you'll also see the third largest cathedral in the world — the "Duomo." It took nearly four centuries to finish this magnificent building ... Can you see why?

Do you have masks?
Here's an Italian mask for you to color.
Go to the next page to see when Italians would usually wear it.

Venice — the city of canals!

Have you heard about **Venice?**
Do you know why it's so special?
Venice is probably the only city in the world where you can cross the road without worrying about looking both ways! 😉 That's because no cars are allowed in the city. Venice is located at the northeast edge of Italy. It sits in a lagoon on the Adriatic Sea. The city is made of more than 100 tiny islands. It's a unique city with **charming canals** of water.

So how do people get from one point to another?
They use the many footbridges and boat canals inside Venice.
The most famous way to travel is by **gondola** — that's a narrow black boat with a flat bottom and a high prow (or bow). One or two oarsmen guide it!

Did you know?
There are 400 footbridges and 170 boat canals that connect the city of Venice!

Water levels in the lagoon are rising, and that creates some problems … Every year, Venice sinks by 1 to 2 millimeters (or about 1/16 of an inch). Often, the city is covered by water during high tide 😯. When that happens, what will you need?
- A sea mask
- Eyeglasses
- A pair of rubber boots

Answer: Rubber boots!

Did you know?
"Carnival" is a celebration where Italians wear masks. It's a time for fun and tricks. A famous Italian saying, "A carnevale ogni scherzo vale," means "At Carnival, every prank goes!"

Have you worn a mask? When do you usually wear it?
If you were in Italy in February, you could wear a mask at a very famous Carnival in Venice. People in **Venetian masks** walk around the canals and stand in the huge St. Mark's Square, which has many pigeons!!

Naples — the world's best pizza!

In **Naples,** you can eat the best pizza on earth! And the famous Mount Vesuvius looks over the city. Naples is the main city in southern Italy. It's located on the amazing Amalfi Coast. This coastline looks like a picture postcard with its steep cliffs, pastel-colored villages, and sparkling turquoise water. Naples is rich in art, music, and tradition. The theater of puppets is very popular here. One of the most loved symbols of Naples is Pulcinella — a funny puppet with large white clothes and a black mask with a curved nose!

Did you know?

Mount Vesuvius is one of three volcanoes in mainland Europe that are still active. But it hasn't erupted since 1944.
In ancient times, it erupted and caused a big earthquake that completely destroyed two cities: Pompeii and Herculaneum.

Quizzes!

1. What is the second most populated city in Italy?

2. Where is the Tower of Giotto?

3. Which city is called "Eternal" or the "Open-Air Musem"?

4. What city is found near an active volcano?

5. What is the Carnival?

6. What city is sinking every year?

Answers:
1. Milan
2. Florence
3. Rome
4. Naples
5. An Italian celebration with masks
6. Venice

Flags, symbols, and coins

This is the tricolor (three-colored) flag of Italy. It's called *bandiera italiana* or *tricolore* in Italian.

Each color has a meaning:
Green stands for Hope and for the plains of Italy.
White stands for Faith and for the snow-capped Alps.
Red stands for Charity (love and kindness) and for the blood shed by those who fought for Italy's independence.

Did you know?
Italians are very proud of their flag. They respect and honor it as the most important symbol of their country.
If you buy an Italian flag, remember that the flag should never be allowed to drag along the ground!

This emblem is the official symbol of Italy. It has a white star with a thin red border. The star's background is a cogwheel with five spokes. It's surrounded by two branches. Can you recognize what trees the branches represent?

Answer:
An olive tree and an oak tree

The Italian wolf is the animal symbol of Italy.

Get to know the COINS OF ITALY ...

Italy is part of the European Union. The country has replaced its own coins (*lira*) with euro coins since 2001. The Italian euro coins are easy to recognize because they show famous Italian art and places. Every coin has the letters "RI" for *Repubblica Italiana* (Italian Republic) and the letter "R" for Rome.

The most famous coin is worth one euro. This coin shows Leonardo da Vinci's drawing called *Vitruvian Man*.

Quizzes!

You want to buy a slice of pizza, and it costs 2.35 euros. How many coins will you have to use if you have only 5-cent euro coins?

Answers: 47 coins

What Italian coins match the sizes below? Place coins on the circles and find the right answers!

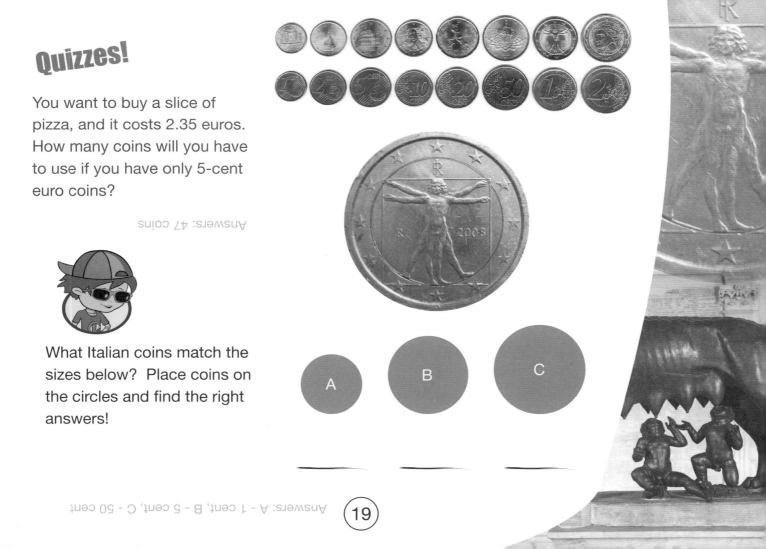

Italy's LONG and SPECIAL history

Italy has a long history! Around 2,000 BC,* tribes of shepherds and farmers lived in little villages in Italy. These villages were often built on the banks of a river or in a fertile valley. Italy was very rich in natural resources, and its land was planted to grow everything necessary!

*BC stands for "before Christ," and AD means "after Christ." AD is short for the Latin phrase *anno Domini.* It means "in the year of the Lord's birth."

One of the small villages was **Rome**. According to a legend, twin brothers **Romulus and Remus** wanted to build a city, but they argued over where it should be. Romulus killed his brother and named the city after himself 😮. Then he declared himself the first King of Rome.

The village of Rome was founded on the banks of the River Tiber in 753 BC. The village soon become a large town. It spread over the surrounding territory and all of Italy. During the next centuries, Rome grew into what is known as the **Roman Empire**.

The Roman Empire covered most of the known world in its time, as you can see on the map!

Compare the borders of Italy today with the Roman Empire! What modern countries would be part of Italy if it was still as big as the ancient Roman Empire?

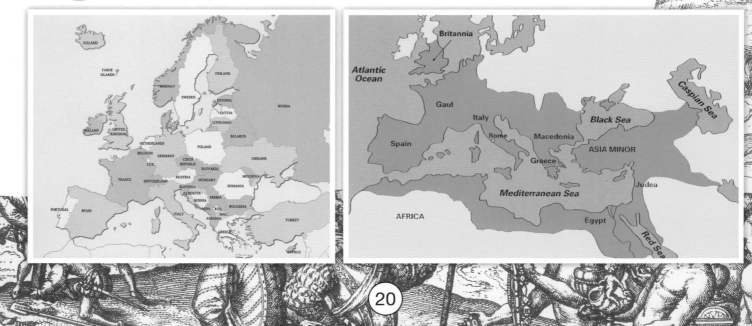

The mighty Roman Empire

Quizzes!

The Roman Empire covered
- 322 km (200 miles).
- 3.7 million km (2.3 million miles).
- The distance between the sun and the moon.

It had a population of
- 10,000 people.
- 5 billion people.
- 120 million people.

Answers:
3.7 million km (2.3 million miles)
120 million people

Many leaders contributed to the growth of Rome and the power of the Roman Empire.
But **Julius Caesar** was definitely the most famous leader in the history of ancient Rome!

Julius Caesar was a great general who helped to expand the boundaries of Rome.

He was born in 100 BC, and he began his career when he was still a teenager. He conquered all of the land that is now France and Belgium, and he invaded Britain twice.

At that time, the Roman Empire was a democratic republic. But Julius Caesar became so powerful that he made himself the master of Rome. In 44 BC, he was killed by people who wanted to free Rome from his control.

From Caesar to modern Italy ...

Did you know?
The month of July was named to honor Julius Caesar. While Caesar was the master of Rome, he created the calendar we use today! He made the year 365 days long, with 366 days in leap years. He decided to start the year with the month of January.

Veni, vidi, vici: These are the famous Latin* words that Julius Caesar used to describe one of his fastest victories.
What do they mean?
- I came, I saw, I conquered.
- I played, I ate, I slept.
- I dreamt, I woke up, I sneezed.

*Latin was the language spoken during the time of the Roman Empire.

Answer: I came, I saw, I conquered.

The Roman Empire in Italy ended in 493 AD. Italy was invaded and conquered by people coming from northern and western Europe.
They divided Italy into many separate kingdoms. The city of Rome was ruled by the Pope, the head of the Catholic Church. The Popes were really like kings. They often entered battles to keep their land and their authority.

In 1861, Italy was officially re-united under a single king.
And in 1870, the state of Rome was conquered and added to the kingdom of Italy.
Italy was a kingdom until 1946. Then after World War II, it became the republic it is today.

What's the difference between a kingdom and a republic?

A kingdom is a country ruled by a king or a queen. In a kingdom, the power passes to the king or queen's son or daughter, or to other members of the royal family. A republic is a country that is governed by representatives who are elected by the citizens.

One of the most talented people of all time: Leonardo da Vinci

Leonardo is very proud to introduce you to Leonardo da Vinci. He is known to be one of the most talented and intelligent people of all time. Leonardo da Vinci was an excellent artist, a great scientist, and a creative inventor!

Did you know?
Leonardo da Vinci studied the flight of birds to draw plans for flying machines that resembled today's helicopters. But he couldn't build them because the technology needed didn't exist at that time.

Mirror writing
Leonardo da Vinci often wrote in the opposite direction to what is normal. This is called "mirror writing," because you need a mirror to read it! He may have written that way because he was left-handed — or because he wanted to hide his ideas from others.

Can you read this mirror writing?　　!trams yrev si odranoeL

Fun activity!
Write a secret message in mirror writing and send it to your friends!

Did you know?
Leonardo da Vinci invented the first bicycle!

Answer: Leonardo is very smart!

Leonardo da Vinci was a kind person! He liked to buy caged birds so he could set them free.

OUR Leonardo is also curious, smart, and an animal lover. He has made many new discoveries around the world that he likes to share with you. That's why our flying friend is named Leonardo too!

Nice to meet you ...
Giuseppe Garibaldi

Many people tried to unite Italy into one kingdom. **Giuseppe Garibaldi** was the most popular leader of the struggle to unite the country. He and his soldiers fought successfully to unite Italy under the rule of one royal family (called House of Savoy).

The volunteers that followed Giuseppe Garibaldi in his battle wore shirts that were which color? (Hint: See Garibaldi's picture at the bottom of the page.)
- Green
- Red
- Purple

Answer: Red

Did you know?

Giuseppe Garibaldi was called the "Hero of Two Worlds." That's because he was also an outstanding soldier in South America, where he fought with rebel groups in Brazil and Uruguay.

Garibaldi's most important victory was called the "Expedition of the Thousand" (or *Spedizione dei Mille* in Italian). He led 1,000 volunteers to conquer the island of Sicily in 1860. A great conquest!

Garibaldi called his horse "Marsala" — the name of the city where he landed in Sicily!

We have talked a lot about Italy, now let's talk about the Italian people …

ITALIANS and their culture

Italians are famous for being friendly and welcoming. They are very devoted to their families and friends. They like **being outdoors** to enjoy Italy's many **sunny days.**

Italians create lots of occasions to eat together, sing together, and play with children!

Playing football* is the most popular way to have fun with friends and parents! Even if you don't speak a word of Italian, it doesn't matter. If you are in a park or public garden, you'll always find someone to play football with you!

*Italian football is the game that is called soccer in North America.

Do you play football (soccer)? _____

What is your favorite team? _____

Do you know any famous Italian football players?

_____

Did you know?

Most Italian people have the same habit. They talk with their hands as much as with their mouths. They use a lot of gestures. Sometimes you can tell what they're saying even if they don't speak English!

Quizzes!

What does the common Italian gesture shown in the picture mean?

- Shall we go!
- Shut up!
- What are you saying??

Answer: What are you saying???

Are you superstitious?

Do you have a good luck charm?

Italians tend to be very superstitious … They believe that some things can bring good luck — and that other things cause bad luck! What do Italians say you must always carry with you for good luck?
A clue … It has the shape of a chili pepper!
- One tail
- One red glass
- One red *corno* ("horn")

And don't forget that in Italy, walking under a ladder is thought to bring bad luck … It's better to go around! 😮

Palio di Siena

Italians are very proud of their traditions, and they hold huge events to remember and honor special dates in Italy's history.

One of the most important celebrations is the Palio di Siena. This was an ancient horse race that is still run today. It follows the same rules as it did eight centuries ago.

Palio di Siena takes place two times during the summer (on July 2 and August 16). The race and four-day celebration are held in the city of Siena, which is in Tuscany in central Italy. The people of Siena take the event very seriously. The rivalry is fierce because every horse in the race belongs to one of the city's districts (or *contrade* in Italian).

The people of Siena say: *"Il palio dura tutto l'anno."* ("Palio lasts all year.") That's because they think about it and prepare for it all year long.

If a district doesn't win the race for many years, the Italians nickname it *Nonna.* (That means "Grandma" in Italian.)

Did you know?
Sometimes the jockeys are thrown off of the horses, but even a horse without a jockey (called *cavallo scosso* in Italian) can win the race for its district!

Famous Italians you might know

Many Italian artists are world famous for their masterpieces, like Leonardo da Vinci, Michelangelo, and Giotto.

Italians are also famous for their inventions and discoveries.

Christopher Columbus was an Italian sailor who was born in the city of Genova. He wanted to find a better way to get to eastern Asia by sailing west around the world. He never knew that he had landed on a new continent instead: "The New World."

What was the continent discovered by
Columbus that was called "The New World"?

- Africa
- Asia
- America

Answer: America. This continent was named after the Italian explorer Amerigo Vespucci.

Marco Polo was a merchant from Venice. He lived from 1254 to 1324. Marco Polo traveled a lot in order to trade goods. When he returned, he told the Italians about China and Indonesia — a part of the world that was unknown at that time.

Amerigo Vespucci was born in Florence in 1454. He sailed the same route as Columbus. But Amerigo Vespucci was the first explorer to realize that he hadn't landed in India, but in "The New World."

Did you know?
An Italian monk named Savino D'Armate invented eyeglasses in the 13th century. The eyeglasses sat on the nose, since frames weren't added until much later.

What is the fairy tale most loved by Italians? It's one you probably know: the story of **Pinocchio**, the wooden puppet who wants to become a real boy. To reach his dream, he has to deserve it … which means he has to stop telling lies!

What happens when Pinocchio tells a lie?

- He becomes short.
- His nose quickly grows.
- He loses his hand.

Answer: His nose quickly grows!

Buon appetito!
Enjoy Italian food!

Italy probably has more different dishes than any place in the world. You'll surely want to taste the pasta, pizza, and gelato … But you'll find that it's difficult to choose with so many types of food 😊!

Did you know?
There are more than 1,000 kinds of pizza in Italy? Let's go discover some of them!

Pizza was invented in the city of Naples around 1860. A baker named Raffaele Esposito prepared the first type of pizza to honor the Queen of Italy at that time — Margherita di Savoia. He made the pizza with ingredients that were the same colors as the Italian flag. He named his pizza Margherita, after the Queen. Help Leonardo find which ingredients match the colors of the Italian flag.

White is _____
Red is _____
Green is _____

Answers:
Mozzarella is white.
Tomatoes are red.
Basil is green.

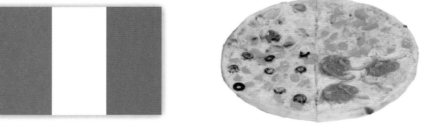

The base for Italian pizza is a **very thin** flat bread. It is loaded with fresh vegetables or thinly sliced ham or salami. Other popular toppings are artichokes, garlic, tomatoes, or olives. There are even pizzas topped with eggs! The pizzas are **baked in a wood-fired oven.**

What is a shop where you can buy pizza called?
A *pizzeria*! Here you can sit and eat a circle pizza. If you want to eat some pizza while you are walking, you have to ask for a slice of pizza at a *pizzerie al taglio*. That's a shop that sells pizza in slices.

Ready to learn about different kinds of pizza? Mmm ...
Leonardo's mouth is watering!

Here are some famous kinds of pizza with their ingredients. Can you match each type of pizza with the right picture? Look at the ingredients shown in the photos!

A. Pizza Marinara

Ingredients: Oil, tomato, garlic, and oregano. It is named "marinara" because it was originally taken along on voyages so that sailors (or *marinai*) could eat pizza during the journey.

B. Pizza Napoletana (Naples)

Ingredients: Tomatoes, mozzarella, anchovies, and capers.

C. Pizza Capricciosa

Ingredients: Mushrooms, ham, artichoke hearts, olives, and half of a hard-boiled egg.

D. Pizza Quattro Stagioni (Pizza Four Seasons)

The ingredients are divided into four sections, one for each season: Spring (olives and artichokes); summer (peppers); autumn (tomato and mozzarella); winter (mushrooms and hard-boiled eggs).

E. Pizza Ai Quattro Formaggi (Pizza with Four Cheeses)

Ingredients: Mozzarella and three local cheeses, such as Gorgonzola, ricotta, and parmigiano-reggiano.

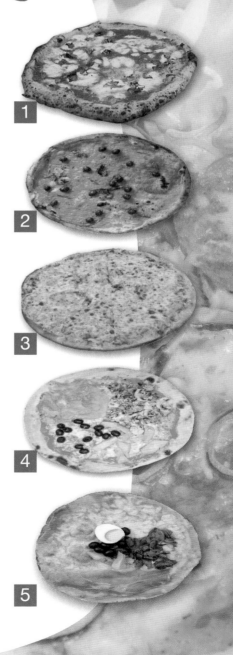

Answers: A-2; B-1; C-5; D-4; E-3

Don't forget to try
Italian spaghetti!

Look at this picture … Yes, it's a fabulous dish of spaghetti — the most well-known type of pasta in Italy.

Pasta is an ancient food, made with four simple ingredients: water, flour, semolina (hard grains left after flour is milled), and salt.

Sometimes eggs are added to create *pasta all'uovo* ("pasta with eggs"). This is common in the northern part of Italy.

What is the right way to eat spaghetti?
It's not easy to eat spaghetti using only a fork, but that's the Italian way — and you can learn it! Simply pick up the right amount of spaghetti, roll it around on your fork, and reach your mouth as soon as possible 😋 !

capelli d'angelo   spaghetti

lasagne   manicotti

elbow   farfalle   ruote

rigatoni   conchiglie   rotini

Help Leonardo connect the pictures to the right type of Italian pasta shown above!

 You can use pasta to create dazzling jewelry. Put the pasta (for example, rigatoni) into a ziplock bag with food coloring. Close the bag and shake it until the pasta is colored. Take the pasta out of the bag and let it dry on a paper towel. After that, you can use the pasta for your creations! Put it on a string to make a colorful necklace or bracelet!

Will you be able to eat it
BEFORE IT MELTS?

What is another tasty Italian delight that you can't miss? Some hints:

- It's not hot.
- It is made of milk.
- It's frozen.

Answer: It's gelato!

There are several types of gelato, with many different flavors to choose from, such as fresh fruit, chocolate, and hazlenut!

Gelato is served in a cone or in a cup. You can get up to FOUR flavors in one cone! But be careful not to stain your clothes — G _____ O melts very fast!

Do you prefer a cone or a cup? Why?

You can ask for a gelato in special shops called *gelateria* in Italian. You'll see all the flavors of gelato you can choose right in the shop window.

There is another frozen dessert Italians love: *granita*! It's made of coarse ice, sugar, and flavorings. And you don't need to worry about stains: you drink it with a straw …

The foods I ate in Italy ...

What is your favorite Italian food?

_____

Have you ever tasted it before?

_____

Quizzes!

If you went with Leonardo to an Italian restaurant, which of these foods would you be most likely to find on the menu?
- ✓ Cheeseburgers
- ✓ Spaghetti
- ✓ Fish and Chips

Answer: Spaghetti

Paste a picture of your favorite Italian food here as a souvenir!

Pizza is made with this basic ingredient:
- ✓ Rice
- ✓ Flat bread
- ✓ Meat

Answer: Flat bread

What is the food you can eat in a cone or in a cup?
- ✓ Gelato
- ✓ Rigatoni
- ✓ Pizza

Answer: Gelato

Leonardo has just landed in Italy, and he wants to taste some new foods.
Can you help him?

1. Where can he find a slice of pizza?

2. Where can he eat a dish of spaghetti?

3. Where can he taste a gelato?

Answers:
1. Pizzeria
2. Ristorante, or osteria or trattoria
3. Gelateria

How do you say it in Italian ...?

A handy dictionary *especially* for you!

It's not hard to recognize the Italian language.

The pronunciation is soft and musical. That's why Italian is used for opera (a type of play where the words are sung instead of spoken).

Do you want to feel a little independent and speak some Italian yourself?

Here are a few common Italian words and how to pronounce them!

Did you know?
There are many local dialects (or differences in how things are said), depending on the region of the country.

Italian word	How does it sound?	What it means in English
Ciao	chow	Hello
Buon giorno	bwon zhor-no	Good morning
Buona sera	bwoh-nah say-rah	Good evening
Arrivederci	ah-ree-vuh-dehr-chee	Bye-bye/see you
Si	see	Yes
No	no	No
Prego	preh-goh	Please
Grazie	graht-zee-ay	Thank you
Grazie mille	graht-zee mee-lay	Thank you very much
Di niente	dee nee-ehn-teh	You're welcome
Scusa	skoo-zah	Excuse me
Mi dispiace	mee dee-spyah-cheh	Sorry
Non parlo Italiano	nohn par-lo ee-tahl-ee-ah-no	I do not speak Italian
Parli Inglese?	par-lee een-gleh-zay	Do you speak English?
Mi chiamo _____.	mee kee-ah-mo	My name is _____.
Come ti chiami?	KOH-meh tee kee-AH-mee	What's your name?

Words to use at the restaurant ...

Family competition!
Who remembers more Italian words?
Test each other ... The winner is the
person who remembers at least five
words with no mistakes!

Restaurant	Ristorante	ri-sto-ràn-te
Breakfast	Colazione	koh-lah-tsee-oh-nay
Lunch	Pranzo	prawn-tsoh
Dinner	Cena	che-nah
Milk	Latte	lah-tay
Bread	Pane	pah-nay
Cup	Tazza	tatz-zah
Glass	bicchiere	bik-kier-ay
Fork	Forchetta	for-ket-tah
Knife	Coltello	kol-tell-oh
Spoon	Cucchiaio	koo-chee-ya-choh
Sugar	Zucchero	sukh-keh-roh
Wine	Vino	vee-noh
Salt	Sale	saa-lay
Pepper	Pepe	pay-pay
Cake	Dolce	dole-chay
Honey	Miele	myeh-lay
Eggs	Uova	u-o-vah
Salad	Insalata	een-sah-lah-tah, een-sah-lah-teh
Beef	Vitello	vee-tehl-loh
Lamb	Agnello	ahn-nyel-loh
Pork	Maiale	mah-yah-lay
Steak	Bistecca	bee-steh-kah
Chicken	Pollo	pohl-loh
Noodles	Spaghetti	spah-geht-tee
Pasta	Pasta	pah-stah
Cheese	Formaggio	for-mah-joh
The bill	Il conto	Il kon-to
piece/slice	Pezzo/fetta	pett-so/feht-tah

Need to BUY something?

Learn Italian numbers!

One	Uno	Oo-noh
Two	Due	Doo-ay
Three	Tre	Tray
Four	Quattro	Kwaht-troh
Five	Cinque	Cheen-kway
Six	Sei	Say-ee
Seven	Sette	Set-tay
Eight	Otto	Oht-toh
Nine	Nove	Noh-vay
Ten	Dieci	Dee-ay-chee
One hundred	Cento	Chen-toh
One thousand	Mille	Meel-lay

 Try to complete the sentences with the correct words in Italian:

There is _____ (*one fork*) on the table, and I want to use it to eat _____ (*three pieces of cake, please*).

Sentences that will come in handy in Italy ...

Here are some important sentences for tourists to know in Italian. Practice them to help you memorize the words:

✓ In English — "Excuse me, I don't speak Italian."

In Italian — Scusami, io non parlo Italiano.

✓ In English — "How much is the ticket to the Metro (the subway)?"

In Italian — Quanto costa un biglietto per la Metro?

✓ In English — "Good evening, where is the train station?"

In Italian — Buona sera, dove si trova la stazione dei treni?

✓ Say your home phone number in Italian numbers.

✓ Count from 1 to 10 in Italian.

✓ Say your hotel room number in Italian.

Have you heard some Italian words that you'd like to learn? Write the words and their meanings here:

1. Example: *porta* means "door"

2. _____

3. _____

4. _____

5. _____ and so on ...

Italy is famous for ...

A leaning tower. It's not the Leaning Tower of Pizza 😉 — it's the Leaning Tower of Pisa (peeza). This marble tower was started in the year 1173, and took over 300 years to finish! But there was a problem …
The ground underneath the tower was too soft to support its weight. Shortly after it was built, the tower began to tilt. It now leans by almost 5 meters (more than 16 feet)!

Did you know?
There is a bell chamber at the top of the tower. Each bell is tuned to a note of the musical scale:
C, D, E, F, G, A, B
How many bells are there?

Answer: Seven

The most popular sport in Italy is football (soccer). Italy has won four World Cups — the last one was in 2006. What is the color of the national team and of the uniforms of the Italian athletes?

Answer:
Azzurro ("light blue"). Often the Italian football team is called *Gli Azzurri* by Italians.

Can you recognize this car? Hint: It's one of the famous sports cars produced in Italy.

Ferrari, along with Lamborghini, Alfa Romeo, and Maserati, are Italian luxury sports cars. They are used in car racing, where they can go over 200 mph!
Ferrari is the most well-known Italian car manufacturer in the world.

More FUN FACTS about Italy!

Italy has the most hotel rooms of any European nation 😯.

Sixty percent of all the world's art treasures are in Italy.

Italians eat 25 kg (55 lbs) of pasta per person every year. That's a lot of pasta!

Up and down …
Italy holds the Guinness record for having the most elevators.

The highest point in Italy is Mont Blanc, in the Alps. It's 4,807 meters (or almost 3 miles) high! 😯

The longest river in Italy is the Po.

The oldest olive tree in Italy grows in the Umbria region. It is said to be over 1,700 years old!

Over 75 percent of Italy is covered with mountains or hills.

No other country in Europe has as many active volcanoes as Italy. The reason is that the Italian peninsula stands on a fault line. Three major volcanoes (Etna, Stromboli, and Vesuvius) have erupted in the last 100 years.

What do you know about Italy?

1. On what continent is Italy located? _____

2. Italy is shaped like what object? _____

3. What natural border separates Italy from other countries in the north?
_____

4. True or false? Po is the name of a river. _____

5. What independent countries are located inside the boundaries of Italy? _____

6. Where is the Vatican City? _____

7. What is the Italian flag called? _____

8. What colors appear on the Italian flag? What do the colors mean?
_____

_____

9. What type of money does Italy use? _____

10. Which Italian city is gradually sinking? _____

11. Complete this sentence: "*Veni, vidi,* _____."
("I came, I saw, _____.")

Answers:
1. Europe
2. Boot
3. Italian Alps
4. True
5. The Republic of San Marino and the Vatican City
6. In Rome
7. Tricolore
8. White, Red, and Green. White stands for Faith and the snow-capped Alps; Green for Hope and the plains; and Red for Charity and the blood shed to win Italy's independence.
9. Euro coins
10. Venice
11. "Vici" ("I conquered.")

39

SUMMARY OF THE TRIP

We had great fun — what a pity it is over ...

Which places did you visit?

_____

_____

Whom did you meet ...

Did you meet tourists from other countries? Yes / No

If you did meet tourists, where did they come from? (Name their nationalities):

_____

Shopping and souvenirs ...

What did you buy on the trip?

_____

What did you want to buy, but ended up not buying?

_____

Experiences

What are the most memorable experiences of the trip?

_____

_____

_____

Record each family member's favorite places:

—————————— : ——————————————
—————————— : ——————————————
—————————— : ——————————————
—————————— : ——————————————

Grade the most beautiful places and the best experiences of your journey:

First place

Second place		Third place

And now, a difficult task — discuss it with your family and decide ...

What did you enjoy most on the trip?

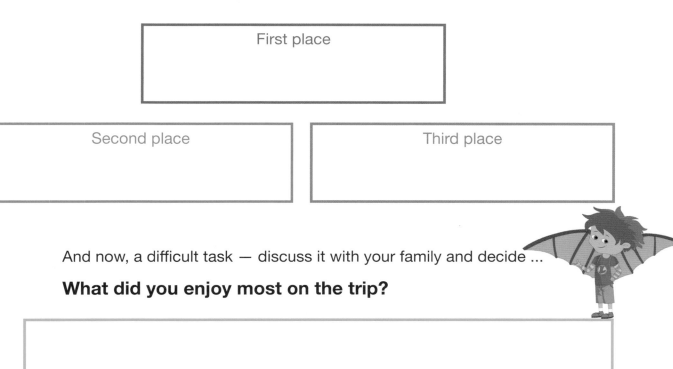

A journal

Which places did
we visit?

What did we do?

A journal

Which places did we visit?

What did we do?

SURPRISE YOUR KIDS
WITH LEONARDO'S PERSONAL GIFTS!

Every week Leonardo sends prizes (backpacks, posters, stickers, and more) to a few lucky children who read our books. New winners each week!

Just send your email address to enter your child in the drawing. PLUS—each child entered will immediately receive a free Kids' Travel Kit and a 25% off promo code for your next journey with FlyingKids®.

Leonardo wants to make your kids happy!
Sign up today at www.theflyingkids.com/happybuyers

GET A CHANCE TO WIN

ENJOY MORE FUN ADVENTURES WITH LEONARDO AND FlyingKids®

Find more Guides to many destinations at www.theflyingkids.com

Get lots of information about family travel, free activities, and special offers

FlyingKidsForYou   @FlyingKidsForYou   @TheFlyingKids1